KU-688-305

Louis
PASTEUR

Liz Gogerly

HODDER
Wayland

an imprint of Hodder Children's Books

C 01 0387107

© 2001 White-Thomson Publishing Ltd

Produced for Hodder Wayland by
White-Thomson Publishing Ltd
2/3 St Andrew's Place
Lewes
BN7 1UP

Editor: Polly Goodman
Designer: Derek Lee
Picture Researcher: Shelley Noronha, Glass Onion Pictures
Cover and Title Page Illustrator: Richard Hook
Science Panel Illustrator: Derek Lee
Map Illustrator: Tim Mayer
Consultant: Dr Brian Bowers, Senior Research Fellow at the
Science Museum, London.
Proofreader: Kay Barnham

Published in Great Britain in 2001 by Hodder Wayland, an imprint
of Hodder Children's Books.
This paperback edition published in 2002.

The right of Liz Gogerly to be identified as the author of this work
has been asserted by her in accordance with the Copyright, Designs
and Patents Act 1988.

All rights reserved. No part of this publication may be reproduced,
stored in a retrieval system, or transmitted, in any form or by any
means without the prior written permission of the publisher, nor
be otherwise circulated in any form of binding or cover other than
that in which it is published and without a similar condition being
imposed on the subsequent purchaser.

British Library Cataloguing in Publication Data
Gogerly, Liz
Louis Pasteur. – (Scientists Who Made History)
1. Pasteur, Louis 2. Chemists – France
1. Title
540.9'2

ISBN 0 7502 3889 5

Printed and bound in Italy by G. Canale & C.S.p.A, Turin

Hodder Children's Books
A division of Hodder Headline Limited
338 Euston Road, London, NW1 3BH

Picture Acknowledgements: AKG 11, 24, 31, 36, 41b; Ann Ronan 16,
17, 21, 23, 28, 34, 35; Bridgeman 7b; Bruce Coleman 30; Florence
Nightingale Museum Trust 6; Institut Pasteur 4, 15, 29, 39b; Hodder
Wayland Picture Library 5, 8b, 25; Hulton Getty 8t, 9, 38, 41t; Mary
Evans 14, 20, 22, 26, 27, 32 Popperfoto 12, 40, 43; Science Photo
Library 10, 13, 18, 19, 33, 37, 39t, 42t & b; Wellcome Institute for
the History of Medicine 7t.

Contents

A Life-and-death Situation

ON 6 JULY 1885 it was just another hot and sticky day in Paris. Louis Pasteur was deep in thought in his laboratory on the outskirts of the city. He had spent five, long years researching rabies and today, out of the blue, his cure for this horrible disease was about to be put to the test.

Earlier that day, a hysterical mother had brought her nine-year-old son, Joseph Meister, to his laboratory. The child had screamed in agony as Pasteur inspected his awful injuries. Joseph had fourteen dog bites and his leg was nearly severed from his body. But there was worse – the dog that had attacked the boy had been rabid and Joseph was sure to die. In desperation, Joseph's mother brought him to Pasteur in the hope that he could save her son.

Pasteur was nervous. It felt too early to try the vaccine because it had not been tested properly. He had tried it on dogs, but never on human beings. If the boy died, Pasteur's reputation as a scientist would be in tatters. What was more, if the child died he could be charged with murder. But this was a life-and-death situation. His colleague, Doctor Vulpian, had agreed that there was nothing but to try and save the boy by injecting him with a course of the rabies inoculations over ten days.

LEFT: *A photograph of Louis Pasteur in 1884. By this time, Pasteur had already been working on the vaccine for rabies for four years. It would be another year before he discovered the cure.*

LEFT: *An engraving showing Pasteur watching as Joseph Meister is given another injection for rabies. It is said that Pasteur suffered from terrible nightmares while he waited for the vaccine to work.*

Being brave

Young Joseph was terrified of the huge needle and winced as the vaccine was injected into his vein. Time crept by slowly, and the day somehow grew longer. Eventually the boy's deep sleep seemed to indicate that the cure was starting to work, but no one knew for sure. For Pasteur there would be no sleep tonight – and possibly none until the ten days were over and Joseph was well again. After twelve days, Pasteur could relax – Joseph had developed none of the symptoms of rabies. What was more, Pasteur had discovered the first-ever vaccine for the disease.

IN THEIR OWN WORDS

'I have not yet dared to treat human beings after bites from rabid dogs; but the time is not far off, and I am much inclined to begin by myself – inoculating myself with rabies, and then arresting the consequences; for I am beginning to feel very sure of my results.'

LOUIS PASTEUR IN A LETTER TO HIS FRIEND JULES VERCEL, ON 28 MARCH 1885.

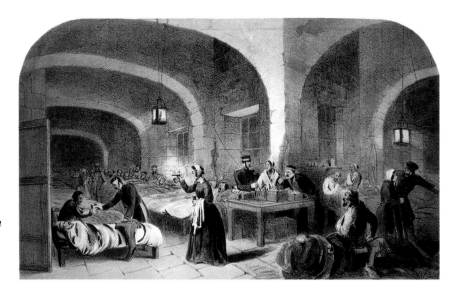

RIGHT: *The English nurse Florence Nightingale helped to improve hospital conditions for soldiers during the Crimean War, which was fought between 1853 and 1856. Her practices revolutionized the nursing profession.*

DEATH, DIRT AND DISEASE

When Louis Pasteur was born, in the early nineteenth century, diseases such as typhoid and cholera killed millions of people around the world. Epidemics of flu, scarlet fever and diphtheria wiped out whole communities. Infection was everywhere and it had many victims. Women often died during childbirth and soldiers frequently died not directly from their wounds, but from infections resulting from them.

Pasteur's world was a very different world to the one we live in today, where we usually feel safe in the hands of doctors and nurses. We expect all hospitals to be clean and free of harmful germs, but in the nineteenth century, people risked their lives by going to hospital, and they didn't realize this until scientists such as Pasteur discovered the truth about germs.

Before Pasteur was born, other scientists had started to make breakthroughs in controlling the spread of disease. The first step against infectious diseases was made in 1796 by an English doctor called Edward Jenner. He discovered the vaccine to prevent smallpox – an infectious, airborne disease that killed hundreds of millions of people, leaving others blind or scarred. Jenner had observed that milkmaids who had suffered from a mild illness called cowpox did not seem to get smallpox. In the course of his experiments, Jenner had injected an eight-year-old boy with cowpox and later injected

RIGHT: *This drawing of Middlesex Hospital, England, in 1808, presents a false impression of hospitals at this time. In reality, such wards were often cramped and dirty, and breeding grounds for disease.*

the same boy with smallpox to prove that he had become immune to this deadly disease. It is the kind of gamble that we find again and again in the history of medicine, and one that Louis Pasteur would take nearly 100 years later.

Jenner paved the way for vaccination. He had opened up ways in which disease could be tackled. But it was the work of Louis Pasteur that brought us a more complete understanding of infection and disease, which in turn led to cures for many more illnesses.

BELOW: *An eighteenth-century cartoon makes fun of Jenner's smallpox vaccination. Inoculation against disease was a strange idea at the time.*

Early Years

LOUIS PASTEUR (pronounced pas-TUR), was born on 27 December 1822 in a small French village called Dôle, near the city of Dijon. He came from an ordinary working family. Louis' father, Jean Joseph, made a living as the village tanner. His mother, Jeanne, was a simple country woman. Pasteur had three sisters and the family lived over the tannery.

Despite his own background, Jean Joseph had aspirations for his son. He wanted Louis to become a teacher at the local school. By the time he was thirteen, Louis showed no outstanding ability in his studies, but he enjoyed fishing and was a talented artist. His pastel portraits of the family impressed his father and for a while the family expected him to become a painter.

About this time, Louis' teacher recognized that he appeared slow in his work only because of the care he took over every detail. This was a turning point in Louis' academic progress. By the time he was fifteen, he was winning school prizes and was encouraged to prepare for the Ecole Normale Supérieure, the national school for the training of college professors in Paris.

ABOVE: *Pasteur was sixteen years old when he drew this life-like pastel drawing of his father, Jean Joseph Pasteur.*

RIGHT: *In this early drawing of his mother, Pasteur shows an artistic talent, which would develop into a sharp scientific eye.*

Map labels:

Lille

UNITED NETHERLANDS

LUXEMBOURG

GERMAN CONFEDERATION

Paris

N

F R A N C E

Strasbourg

BAY OF BISCAY

Dijon • Dôle

Arbois

S W I T Z E R L A N D

A L P S

I T A L Y

0   200   400   600 kilometres
0   200   400 miles

S P A I N

MEDITERRANEAN SEA

ABOVE: *France and its neighbouring countries in 1822, when Pasteur was born.*

BELOW: *The village of Dôle in France, where Pasteur was born.*

Homesick blues

In 1838, Louis left Dôle to go to Paris to study, but almost from the beginning he was homesick. Within a month he was back in Dôle. He felt a failure, but his family and teachers supported him. He spent a few months thinking about what he wanted to do with his life and took time to paint once again. He even sketched the local mayor. Louis then decided to take up his teacher training at the local school. The following year, he attended the college at Besançon, which was 40 kilometres away from Dôle. Louis thrived there and was appointed preparation master. After a false start, Pasteur was on his way.

PARIS, AT LAST!

Pasteur was a serious young man. He was steeped in traditional values, and family loyalty, high morals, dedication to hard work and financial security were his driving forces. His early failure made him even more determined to do well. In the summer of 1842, Pasteur received his baccalauréat in science (the equivalent of A' levels), but his results were only average. He was offered a place at the Ecole Normale in Paris once again, to study to become a science teacher, but he decided he wanted to boost his results before returning there. His only stumbling block was that the additional education he needed could only be found in Paris.

In 1842, Pasteur overcame his fears of homesickness and returned to Paris to attend the Lycée Saint-Louis, a preparatory school for the Ecole Normale. This time he had the companionship of his best friend, Charles Chappuis, who took his rather grave friend out on long walks, or on trips to the theatre. Meanwhile, Pasteur's father would write to Chappuis for information about his son, to check that he wasn't unhappy.

LEFT: *A drawing of Pasteur aged eighteen, while studying at the Ecole Normale Supérieure in Paris.*

His father needn't have worried. Pasteur was entering a new phase in his life. Hard work paid off and at the end of his year at the Lycée Saint-Louis, he won first prize for physics and entered the Ecole Normale in 1843 in fourth place. Pasteur entered the Ecole Normale in his twenty-first year. By the time he left he was twenty-six and had been awarded a Doctor of Science degree (DSc) with a job as chemistry assistant at the college. By this time, the idea of a teaching job near his parents' home had lost its charm and his sights were set on a career in science.

BELOW: *The Boulevard Poissonnière in Paris, in 1835. With its wide boulevards and grand buildings, Paris was quite different to Pasteur's hometown of Dôle.*

IN THEIR OWN WORDS

'*Do not be anxious about my health and work. I need hardly get up till 5.45; you see it is not so very early. I shall spend my Thursdays in a neighbouring library with Chappuis, who has four hours to himself that day. On Sundays we shall walk and work a little together; we hope to do some Philosophy on Sundays, perhaps too on Thursdays; I shall also read some literary works. Surely you must see that I am not homesick this time.*'

LOUIS PASTEUR IN A LETTER TO HIS PARENTS, IN NOVEMBER 1842.

Boulevard

Poissonniere

'I remember hurrying from the laboratory and grabbing one of my chemistry assistants and excitedly telling him that, "I have made a great discovery... I am so happy that I am shaking all over." At this time, I was twenty-five years old and had only been doing research for two years.'

PASTEUR, REMEMBERING HIS DISCOVERIES ABOUT CRYSTALS IN 1847.

THE MYSTERY OF THE CRYSTALS

In 1847, while studying at the Ecole Normale, Louis Pasteur set off on a path of discovery that would bring him into the scientific limelight. As part of his doctoral thesis, he chose to investigate the way crystals affect polarized light (polarized light is light that has vibrations all in one plane, which is called the 'plane of polarization', unlike ordinary light, which has vibrations in all directions). This type of study was a brave undertaking for such a young scientist, but Pasteur was already building a reputation for taking risks.

The study of crystals had been a matter of interest among scientists for many years. The German chemist Eilhardt Mitscherlich had discovered that tartaric acid crystals could be divided into two groups. When polarized light was passed through a crystal from one group, its plane of polarization was turned. When polarized light was passed through a crystal from the other group, the light was turned in the opposite direction.

LEFT: *Eilhardt Mitscherlich (1794–1863) was a German chemist who is best-known for his work on crystals.*

WHAT IS A CRYSTAL?

Many substances are crystalline. Salt and sugar, or jewels such as diamonds are just some of the substances you might know that have a crystalline structure. But it is only under a microscope that the real beauty of a crystal can be appreciated. Hundreds of smooth, flat faces meet at corners and edges to form intricate shapes. These shapes are formed because the atoms and molecules that form the substance are arranged in a regular structure. Each substance has its own special structure, which is why there is such a variety of crystal shapes.

The two groups had exactly the same chemical formula (the molecules of each group contained the same numbers of atoms), yet when he examined the two groups of crystals under the microscope, Pasteur found that the structures of the two groups were different. Crystals in one group were a mirror image of the crystals in the other. Pasteur had found out how two crystals with exactly the same chemical properties can behave differently. Before long, the science world was full of admiration for its talented young protégé. At the age of twenty-six, Pasteur was welcomed into its fold.

ABOVE: *This modern photograph of crystals shown under a microscope reveals the amazing effect of passing polarized light through ascorbic acid. The photograph has been magnified thirty times.*

ABOVE: *A print showing Strasbourg in the 1860s. In the four years he lived in Strasbourg, Pasteur married Marie and had three children.*

A FAMILY MAN

In May 1848, tragedy struck: Pasteur's mother died suddenly from a brain haemorrhage. Pasteur decided he must leave Paris to be near his family so he could support them. In September 1848, he became Professor of Physics at the lycée (college) in Dijon. However, by January 1849 he had taken up a new position as Acting Professor of Chemistry at the Faculty of Sciences, Strasbourg Academy, in eastern France.

Within a month of being at Strasbourg, Pasteur probably made one of the quickest decisions of his life. He met and proposed marriage to 22-year-old Marie Laurent, the daughter of the rector of Strasbourg Academy. Marie had been brought up with the same traditional values as Pasteur's family and he was attracted to her simplicity and loyalty to loved ones. It was clear at once that she was marrying a man who was obsessed with his work. On their wedding day, on

29 May 1849, it is said that Pasteur had to be chased out of the laboratory to get to the ceremony on time. However, Marie would become a patient and understanding partner. She learned about crystals and other aspects of Pasteur's work so that she could help him to prepare papers and assist him in the laboratory.

The five years that Pasteur worked at Strasbourg were happy times. In 1850, the Pasteurs had a daughter called Jeanne. In 1851 they had a son called Jean-Baptiste and in 1853 they had another daughter called Cécile. Pasteur was a devoted father, but family life did not keep him away from the laboratory. By 1854, his work with crystals was coming to an end and he was looking for something new to investigate.

IN THEIR OWN WORDS

'My plan of study is traced for this coming year... I think I have already told you that I am on the mysteries, and that the veil which covers them is getting thinner and thinner. The nights seem to me too long, yet I do not complain, for I prepare my lectures easily, and often have five whole days a week that I can give up to the laboratory. I am often scolded by Madame Pasteur, but I console her by telling her that I shall lead her to fame.'

LOUIS PASTEUR IN A LETTER TO HIS FRIEND, CHARLES CHAPPUIS, IN DECEMBER 1851.

LEFT: *A photograph of Marie Pasteur in 1850, a year after her marriage to Louis. She told her husband, 'You must teach me about everything, so I can help you.' It was a promise she kept faithfully and she often helped Pasteur in the laboratory.*

The Secret of Fermentation

IN THE AUTUMN of 1854, the Pasteurs moved to Lille. Pasteur had been offered the post of Professor of Chemistry and Dean at the new School of Sciences. It was an exciting opportunity which would open up a whole new area of research for Pasteur.

At Lille, Pasteur taught students about sugar-making and refining, and about the fermentation and manufacture of beetroot alcohol. This industry was very important to local businesses and Pasteur found himself increasingly intrigued by this new subject. Then, in 1856, a Lille businessman called Monsieur Bigo approached Pasteur with an interesting problem. Something was going wrong in the production of beetroot alcohol at his factory. The alcohol was turning sour. Once again Pasteur was given a mystery to solve.

BELOW: *This engraving shows the production of beetroot alcohol in France in 1870. When Pasteur first investigated the problems of fermentation in beetroot alcohol, he did it out of concern for the failing beetroot alcohol industry in France. He didn't realize that it would lead him to discover more about the fermentation process in general.*

The little 'creatures'

Pasteur visited Bigo's factory and began to analyse, under the microscope, samples of beetroot juice in various stages of fermentation. He saw how yeast was added to the huge vats of beetroot juice. This created little bubbles, which would rise to the surface of the mixture. The bubbles meant that fermentation had begun, and the beetroot juice would slowly turn into alcohol. By examining the shape of tiny moving particles in the samples, Pasteur found that he could determine whether fermentation would be successful or not. If the particles were rod-shaped, the alcohol would turn sour, but if they were round it would ferment successfully.

By taking regular samples of the beetroot juice and looking at it under the microscope, Pasteur showed Bigo how to add yeast successfully, so that the alcohol would not turn sour. But Pasteur wasn't content to leave it there. The tiny moving particles, or 'creatures', intrigued him. Also, there were too many questions left unanswered about fermentation and, by 1856, his research was centred on the subject.

FERMENTATION

Fermentation is a process where a substance, for example fruit juice, turns into something else once an agent such as yeast is added. People had been producing alcohol, vinegar and bread for centuries using the fermentation process, but nobody really understood it. Before Louis Pasteur's work, scientists believed that fermentation was a chemical process (to do with the arrangement of atoms and molecules) rather than a biological one (to do with plant or animal life). In the production of alcohol, for example, they believed that the yeast and fruit juice chemically reacted with each other to cause fermentation.

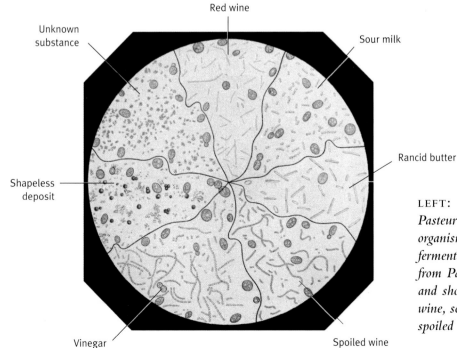

LEFT: *Under the microscope, Pasteur studied all kinds of organisms which caused fermentation. This drawing is from Pasteur's own laboratory and shows fermentation in red wine, sour milk, rancid butter, spoiled wine and vinegar.*

ABOVE: *This drawing shows Pasteur standing in a wine cellar discovering the law of fermentation in wine. Pasteur believed passionately that experimentation in the laboratory and 'in the field' were the ways forward in science. He would spend hours in his laboratory creating variations of the same experiment in order to prove his theories.*

THE TRUTH ABOUT LIVING THINGS

By 1857, Pasteur had published his discoveries about fermentation, which occurred in the creation of many foods and drinks, including wine, beer and also dairy products such as milk and cheese. He deduced that there were two kinds of fermentation: lactic (which occurred with milk and dairy products) and alcoholic (which occurred with wine, beer and vinegar). In alcoholic fermentation, it was the yeast that began the fermentation process. But what was it that caused fermentation in dairy products? Once he could answer this, Pasteur would understand more about fermentation, which would help him to find out why fermentation went wrong in beetroot alcohol production.

The strange grey mould

Pasteur noted that in lactic fermentation, a grey mould appeared that acted like the yeast in alcohol fermentation. The grey mould contained lactic acid, which is the substance that turns milk sour and makes butter go off.

Pasteur went on to find that ruined beetroot alcohol also contained lactic acid. Those tiny, rod-shaped 'creatures' in the beetroot alcohol, which he would later call microbes, were actually the result of lactic fermentation and these were responsible for turning the alcohol sour. This was very interesting – how was this form of fermentation occurring in the alcohol?

Pasteur also found that the yeast in alcohol fermentation was 'living' and the tiny microbes were dividing and multiplying in number. He had proved that fermentation was a biological process to do with 'life', rather than a chemical process. Pasteur was gripped by the subject – he was on to something really big.

In 1857, Pasteur became Administrator and Director of Scientific Studies at the Ecole Normale in Paris. This role meant that he wasn't encouraged to conduct experiments and so he wasn't given a laboratory. However, nothing would deter Pasteur – he was primed for success.

IN THEIR OWN WORDS

'Nothing is more agreeable to a man who has made science his career than to increase the number of discoveries, but his cup of joy is full when the result of his observations is put to immediate practical use.'

LOUIS PASTEUR, DESCRIBING THE SATISFACTION OF PUTTING HIS DISCOVERIES INTO PRACTICE.

ABOVE: *A photograph of wine yeast cells under a microscope, magnified over 800 times. Powerful modern microscopes allow twenty-first-century scientists to see the fermentation process in minute detail. Pasteur did not have the same technology, but he saw the tiny cells of yeast budding off to make smaller 'daughter' cells through his own microscope.*

ABOVE: *The seventeenth-century Dutch naturalist Anton van Leeuwenhoek found microbes in many living things, including tartar found on our teeth.*

TAKING UP THE CHALLENGE

Louis Pasteur wasn't the only scientist interested in microbes. When a Dutchman called Anton van Leeuwenhoek (1632–1723) discovered the microscope at the end of the seventeenth century, he discovered microbes in rainwater. Leeuwenhoek went on to find that all living things are made up of these little creatures.

Spontaneous generation?

Then, in the mid-eighteenth century, an Italian priest called Lazaro Spallanzani (1729–99) took up the subject. At this time most people believed that living things simply came to life when God created them, in a process that later became known as spontaneous generation. For example, they believed that maggots, which they sometimes found in meat, suddenly just appeared. Spallanzani, however, didn't believe that living things simply appeared. He went on to show that maggots hatched out of eggs carried by flies. Spallanzani applied this principle to microbes: they too didn't simply appear – they had to come from somewhere. Like Pasteur, Spallanzani watched microbes dividing and multiplying under the microscope. This was an amazing discovery, but it was almost forgotten until over fifty years later, when Pasteur took up the debate.

IN THEIR OWN WORDS

'Thus, gentlemen, admit the doctrine of spontaneous generation, and the history of creation and the origin of the organic world is no more complicated than this. Take a drop of sea water... that contains some sea mucus, some 'fertile jelly' as it is called, and in the midst of this inanimate matter, the first beings of creation take birth spontaneously, then little by little are transformed and climb from rung to rung – for example, to insects in 10,000 years and no doubt to monkeys and man at the end of 100,000 years.'

LOUIS PASTEUR AT THE SORBONNE, DISPUTING SPONTANEOUS GENERATION ON 7 APRIL 1864.

Rising to the occasion

In December 1859, Felix Pouchet, the director of the Natural History Museum in Rouen addressed the Academy of Sciences in Paris. He claimed that his experiments showed that microbes did just appear and that spontaneous generation was a fact. Pasteur was instantly driven to prove his fellow scientist wrong. A letter from Pouchet to Pasteur challenging him to disprove his theory added fuel to Pasteur's fire. He found a couple of vacant rooms in the Ecole Normale and set up his own laboratory. The small attic rooms were so tiny that he couldn't stand up straight, but he was determined to show the science world that there was no such thing as spontaneous generation. His work with fermentation held the key and the answers were within his grasp.

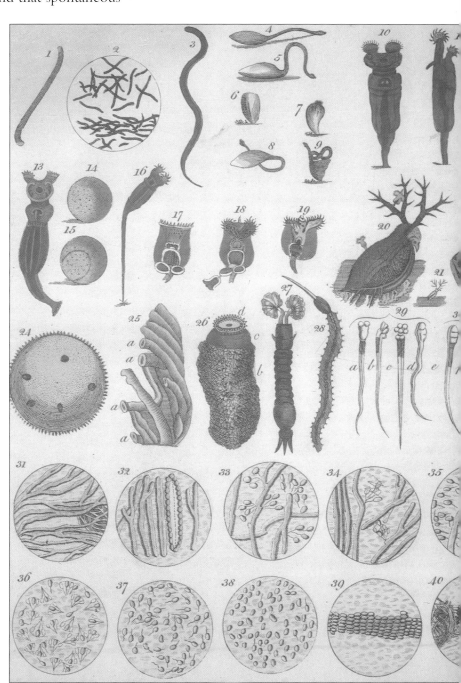

RIGHT: *Leeuwenhoek's discovery of the microscope opened up a whole new world. These drawings, published in 1795, show microscopic creatures invisible to the naked eye, including microbes and insects so small that millions can be found in a circle the same size as the one in the top-left corner of the picture.*

Shaking up the Science World

PASTEUR HAD A hunch — he was sure that microbes were airborne. Perhaps the microbes that created lactic acid in beetroot alcohol came from the air. But how was he going to prove this to a sceptical world who wanted to believe in spontaneous generation?

Pasteur set up a series of experiments. First, he took sugared yeast water and boiled it to kill any microbes it contained. He then poured it into two flasks, and boiled and sterilized them so that the air inside the flasks would also be free of microbes. Finally, he sealed the flasks and waited for a few weeks to see if there were any microbes present. Since all scientific experiments need a control, where the same experiment is set up twice and the differences between them can be compared, Pasteur opened one of the flasks to the air.

The famous experiment

After a few weeks, Pasteur took a sample from each flask and looked at them under a microscope. Despite the absence of microbes in the sealed flask and the presence of microbes in the unsealed flask, Pasteur knew that people would still not be convinced that this wasn't spontaneous generation. He'd have to show that it was something in ordinary air that caused microbes to grow. Back in the laboratory, Pasteur devised a new experiment with swan-necked flasks to show that it was ordinary air, not sterilized air, that caused the microbes to multiply.

BELOW: *This engraving shows Pasteur hard at work in his laboratory. He would go to any length to prove that his experiments in the laboratory would hold up in the 'real world'. Many scientists criticized his showmanship, but for Pasteur these 'events' were calculated risks based on years of painstaking experiments in the laboratory.*

THE SWAN-NECKED FLASKS

To prove that microbes were airborne, Pasteur poured unsterilized, sugared yeast water into flasks. Then he heated the neck of each flask until it melted and could be pulled into shape. He curved the neck downwards and then upwards towards the unsealed end to make a u-bend. The flasks were then boiled to kill the microbes. As the liquid cooled, ordinary air was free to fill the flasks. However, the u-bend in the necks trapped and prevented the microbes from rising up and into the flask. As Pasteur had suspected, the liquid within the flasks remained free of microbes. To show that it was the outside air that created microbes, Pasteur then tipped the flask so that a rush of ordinary air would come into contact with the sterile solution. Once again, Pasteur was proved right. The liquid in these flasks was gradually filled with microbes.

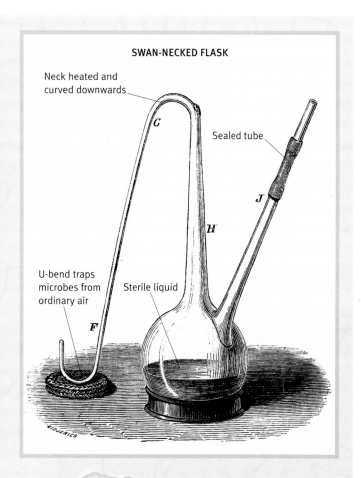

SWAN-NECKED FLASK

Neck heated and curved downwards

G

Sealed tube

J

H

U-bend traps microbes from ordinary air

Sterile liquid

F

To further his evidence, Pasteur took to the streets of Paris. In 1860, he visited different locations and opened his sterile flasks to the air. The results were incredible: the flasks that had been opened in over-crowded areas produced microbes at an alarming rate, whereas the flasks from the laboratory produced very few microbes. Pasteur had disproved spontaneous generation and proved Pouchet wrong. Immediately, Pasteur's thinking began to take him in a new direction: perhaps microbes were the cause of disease in humans and animals? Pasteur started to research what would become his famous germ theory of disease.

ABOVE: *A copy of Pasteur's own drawing of his famous swan-necked flask, which he used to disprove spontaneous generation.*

GERM THEORY PUT TO THE TEST

While on a mission up Mont Blanc in the Alps, in 1860, Pasteur proved that mountain air is healthier than city air. Using his swan-necked flasks, he showed there were fewer microbes in the crisp mountain air than there were in the samples he'd taken in Paris. Of the twenty flasks Pasteur opened at 600 metres up Mont Blanc, only one produced any microbes.

This evidence did not bring the debate on spontaneous generation to an end, but Pasteur was convinced, and in 1862 he was elected to the French Academy of Science. In 1864 he said, 'Life is a germ and a germ is life.' He was saying that germs, or microbes, were everywhere and that they caused fermentation, decay and possibly even disease.

Pasteurization

If Pasteur did not gain everybody's support, he was recognized as a great scientist by most people. In 1864, he was called upon by the French Emperor Napoleon III. The French wine industry was threatened by a disease that turned wine sour. Pasteur quickly recognized the problems the wine-makers were experiencing. Once again, microbes were the issue, and Pasteur needed to find a way of destroying them. Heat destroyed microbes, but he needed to develop a way of heating the wine so that it still tasted good. He found that if the bottled wine was kept at temperatures of between 50–60 °C for a short amount of time, all the microbes would be killed and could not develop again because the bottles were

BELOW: *Napoleon III (1808-73) ruled as Emperor of France from 1852 to 1870. When he asked Pasteur for his help with the struggling French wine industry, Pasteur was honoured and took up the challenge with enthusiasm.*

'If ever you come to Edinburgh, I think you will find it truly rewarding to walk round our hospital and see how greatly mankind is benefiting from your work. Need I add how great a satisfaction I would derive myself from showing you how much the art of surgery is in your debt.'

A LETTER FROM JOSEPH LISTER TO LOUIS PASTEUR IN 1874,
WHILE LISTER WAS PROFESSOR OF SURGERY AT EDINBURGH UNIVERSITY.

BELOW: *A photograph of the British doctor Joseph Lister, aged about forty. Lister, who was known as 'the father of antiseptic surgery', always paid homage to Pasteur. And, like Pasteur, he strongly believed in applying experimental science to the real world.*

already sealed from the air. This system was later called pasteurization after Pasteur, and it is now used to stop beer, milk, cheese and many other foodstuffs from turning sour.

In Britain, the doctor Joseph Lister had also recognized that Pasteur's work was important. In 1865, Lister was Professor of Surgery in Glasgow and from his own experiences, he'd concluded that infection was caused by something in the air. Pasteur's work had inspired him. It led Lister to discover that antiseptics and carbolic acid prevented the spread of infection and germs in hospitals.

BORN TO RESEARCH

Louis Pasteur was a very private man. Amongst the many laboratory notebooks, letters and reports that are housed at the Pasteur Institute in Paris, there is little about Pasteur's homelife or much that reveals his personality. This also reflects how much he dedicated himself to his science.

Pasteur was a workaholic, who rose at dawn to be at his laboratory every day, even on Sundays. His work not only took all his time, but those hours stooped over a microscope influenced the way he behaved. At mealtimes, Pasteur would scrutinize the cutlery to ensure that it was clean and free of microbes. His germ theory meant that he was all too aware of how easily infections could be passed from person to person. For this reason, Pasteur didn't like to shake hands with people, and in Victorian society that must have seemed very rude.

RIGHT: *An engraving from a photograph of a rather stern-looking Pasteur in 1863. At the Ecole Normale, Pasteur had little patience for students who did not abide by the rules. On one occasion, he expelled two students who had left the school for two hours without permission, and he promised to expel anyone caught smoking.*

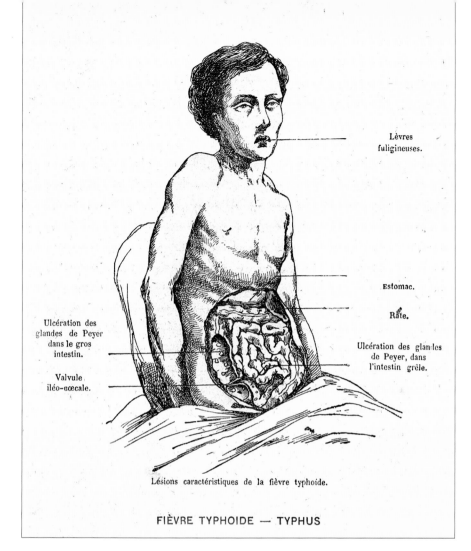

Lèvres fuligineuses.

Estomac.

Rate.

Ulcération des glandes de Peyer dans le gros intestin.

Ulcération des glandes de Peyer, dans l'intestin grêle.

Valvule iléo-cœcale.

Lésions caractéristiques de la fièvre typhoide.

FIÈVRE TYPHOIDE — TYPHUS

LEFT: *This cross-section diagram, drawn in France in about 1880, shows the effects of typhoid fever on a victim, including dark lips and ulcers in the intestine. Typhoid used to be common in all cities and it killed three out of Pasteur's five children. The disease became less common when methods of good hygiene and sanitation were developed.*

Personal tragedy

Just as his work influenced everything he did, Pasteur's personal life occasionally affected his work. In 1859, Pasteur's daughter Jeanne died from typhoid fever. He found comfort in his work, possibly because he felt he was doing something to fight the disease that killed her.

Pasteur wasn't an easy man to live with. He didn't have a sense of humour, he hated lack of discipline and he didn't like to entertain. It was almost as if he was born to research germs. Even his short-sightedness meant that he was able to see things close up in a way that normal-sighted people cannot.

IN THEIR OWN WORDS

'Your father, very busy as always, says little to me, sleeps little, and gets up at dawn – in a word, continues the life that I began with him thirty-five years ago today.'

A LETTER FROM MARIE PASTEUR TO HER DAUGHTER ON HER 35TH WEDDING ANNIVERSARY TO LOUIS.

From Germs to Silkworms

IN JUNE 1865, Pasteur was on another mercy mission. This time his skills were called upon by Jean-Baptiste Dumas, a chemist, politician and close of friend of Pasteur's who lived in Alais, a silkworm region in the south of France. The French silk industry was threatened by a disease called pebrine, which was killing the eggs, chrysalides and the moths that made silk. Pasteur was not a zoologist, nor did he know much about silkworms, but his work on fermentation gave him some confidence. At least he knew something about microbes and germs.

BELOW: *Drawings showing the stages in the silk-making process in the nineteenth century. From top-left, clockwise: gathering mulberry leaves; rearing the silkworms on shelves; reeling silk from the cocoons; weaving; silk clothing; dress-making; selling silk in a shop; silk merchants; a throwing machine (used to make the silk stronger).*

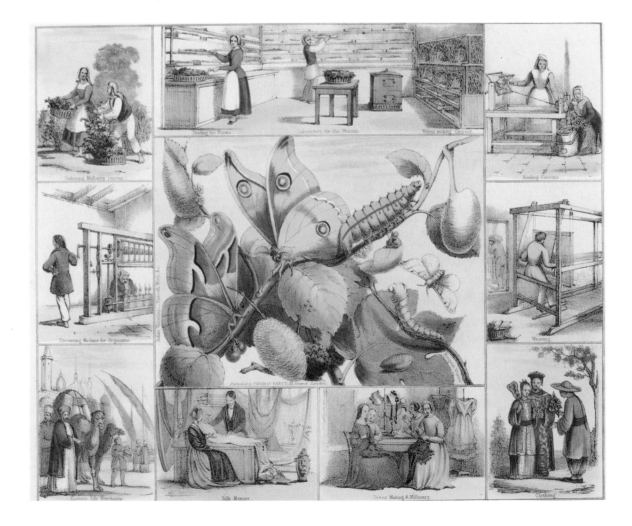

The silkworm farmers described the appearance of the disease: tiny black dots that looked like a sprinkling of ground pepper covered some of the creatures. However, some of the silkworms that appeared to be healthy went on to develop the disease as they changed into moths. Pasteur began to observe these manifestations for himself, but it was difficult to make a full study in the short growing season of the worms. The farmers became desperate for answers and Pasteur began to feel the pressure.

The silkworms' disease was confusing and there didn't seem to be any logic to it. Silkworms covered with the black speckles sometimes survived, whereas silkworms without the blight sometimes became sick. Just as his investigations were getting going, Pasteur received a dreadful telegram – his father was very ill. Pasteur dropped his work and dashed back to Arbois, but his father had already died.

Pasteur managed to throw himself back into his work but in September 1865, tragedy struck again with the death of his two-year-old daughter Camille, who died from a mystery liver disease. This was an awful time for Pasteur, and it seemed that things could not get worse. But early the next year, his twelve-year-old daughter Cécile died from typhoid. It took every bit of Pasteur's determination to return to Alais and continue his work with the silkworms.

ABOVE: *A photograph of three of Pasteur's children in 1862. From the left: Jean-Baptiste, Cécile and Marie-Louise. Four years after this photograph was taken, Cécile tragically died from typhoid fever.*

IN THEIR OWN WORDS

'*Pasteur was everywhere around the tragic silk country, lecturing, asking innumerable questions, teaching the farmers to use microscopes, rushing back to the laboratory to direct his assistants – and in the evenings he dictated answers to letters and scientific papers and speeches to Madame Pasteur. The next morning he was off again to the neighbouring towns, cheering up despairing farmers and haranguing them...*'

FROM *THE MICROBE HUNTERS* BY PAUL DE KRUIF (1926).

IN THEIR OWN WORDS

'Let us therefore strive in the pacific field of Science for the pre-eminence of our several countries. Let us strive, for strife is effort, strife is life when progress is the goal.'

LOUIS PASTEUR, AT AN INTERNATIONAL CONGRESS IN ITALY FOR THE SILK INDUSTRY.

SUCCESS AT A PRICE

In 1867, Pasteur was still investigating the silkworm disease. Eventually he found that the disease was caught through contact with sick worms, or by eating mulberry leaves contaminated by their droppings. If farmers kept sick worms away from healthy ones, the healthy worms would survive.

However, when the next growing season arrived, the worms were still diseased. Pasteur was mystified and the farmers were annoyed – it was a terrible time. He had no choice but to get back to his microscope.

Pasteur had been right to separate the sick worms from the healthy ones, but he went on to discover a second disease in the worms. This disease was called flacherie and, like pebrine, the first disease, it was highly contagious. Again, Pasteur's advice was to separate the sick from the healthy worms. He eventually located a bacteria caused by the

RIGHT: *A healthy mulberry silkworm (larva) spins its cocoon. The silkworm remains in its silky case until it hatches into a moth. Pasteur taught the silk farmers how to use microscopes to determine whether the silkworms were sick or healthy.*

LEFT: *A drawing of Pasteur in his laboratory, in about 1869. Long hours, anxiety about his work, and sorrow for his young family finally affected Pasteur's health when he suffered a stroke at the age of forty-five. After the stroke, he began to look like an old man and needed a stick to help him walk.*

diseases in the bodies of infected silkworms and went on to show the farmers how they could use microscopes to find out which worms were infected. Flacherie bacteria also lived in spores, which are like small sacks containing the microbes in a 'sleeping' state. If the spores were given the right temperature or conditions, they brought the microbes back to life. Pasteur stressed that it was important to keep the silkworms' nurseries clean and dry, with plenty of fresh air. Hot weather and dirty surroundings were the perfect conditions for the microbes to burst back to life and become dangerous.

A near-death experience

In March 1868, Pasteur went back to Alais to find that the silkworms were alive and well. He had saved the silk industry. In the autumn of 1868, he returned to Paris a hero and at the order of Napoleon III, a new laboratory was to be built for him.

Pasteur's joy was short-lived. On 19 October 1868, he woke up with an unusual tingling on his left side. That night the feeling got worse and he suffered a stroke. He was only forty-five years old but everyone, including himself, expected him to die. Pasteur was a born fighter though and by January 1869, he was back at work.

IN THEIR OWN WORDS

'Will I live to finish this work on silkworms? Will I live to discover new mysteries and find these truths which God has created? Have I been able to provide a stone to this edifice of knowledge? I can only hope.'

PASTEUR, JUST AFTER HIS STROKE, IN 1868.

THE FIGHT AGAINST INFECTION

Pasteur's research into the diseases of the silkworms was important to our understanding of disease in general. Pasteur noticed that healthy worms were more likely to fight against the germs that caused the diseases. He found that some worms were struck down by the disease instantly, others lingered for weeks before death, while a few managed to survive. Those that survived lived in cleaner nurseries with adequate sanitation, better food and good ventilation. These might seem simple ideas to us today, but in the mid-nineteenth century, it was groundbreaking in terms of understanding health and the spread of disease.

In 1870, France went to war with Prussia, a German state, and all the other German states joined Prussia. Pasteur, who now had a limp and slight paralysis from his stroke, decided to move back to Arbois, while his son Jean-Baptiste joined the army. The Franco-Prussian War highlighted the need to understand disease. Of 13,000 French soldiers who had surgery during the war, 10,000 died of infection.

BELOW: *Prussian cavalry charge against French infantry in one of the battles of the Franco-Prussian War. France lost many of its sons to war in the nineteenth century. The Napoleonic wars from 1799–1814 were horrific and the dreadful losses during the Franco-Prussian war of 1870–71 made the conditions of injured soldiers a national issue once again.*

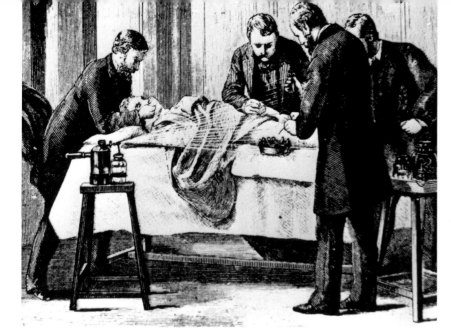

LEFT: *Surgeons in 1870 use an antiseptic spray of carbolic acid to kill bacteria which might enter the wound and cause infection. Pasteur devised this spray for surgeons following antiseptic methods developed in 1867 by Joseph Lister.*

The French doctor Alphonse Guerin started to use antiseptics similar to those used by Joseph Lister, and as a result he saw higher survival rates. Guerin invited Pasteur to his hospital and Pasteur became a regular visitor. By observing medical practice, Pasteur was getting an invaluable insight into disease. He recommended a code of practice for surgeons and nurses, which included heating bandages, washing themselves and sterilizing their instruments. He blamed the epidemic of women dying in childbirth on doctors and nurses who unknowingly spread infectious microbes from one patient to another by not sterilizing themselves or their instruments properly.

'Find the germ!'

Pasteur became more convinced that there was a link between fermentation and disease in man. 'Find the germ!' Pasteur famously once said. When the germ was isolated, he reasoned, a way of controlling or killing it was possible. But the germ for each kind of disease had to be found first.

In 1873, Pasteur was elected to the Academy of Medicine, an exclusive scientific society where new discoveries were presented. This was a great honour. Even though he wasn't a doctor, Pasteur's work was recognized as important to medicine.

IN THEIR OWN WORDS

'If it is a terrifying thought that life is at the mercy of the multiplication of these minute bodies, it is a consoling hope that science will not always remain powerless before such enemies, since for example at the very beginning of the study we find that simple exposure to air is sufficient at times to destroy them.'

LOUIS PASTEUR IN *THE GERM THEORY AND ITS APPLICATION TO MEDICINE AND SURGERY* (1878)

Vaccinations Discovered

PASTEUR WORKED HARD researching theories about germs, but there was a huge number of different kinds of germs to investigate. Luckily, chance intervened. In 1878, Pasteur received a strange 'gift' from Monseur Toussaint at the veterinary school in Toulouse. Toussaint gave Pasteur the head of a chicken that had died from chicken cholera. What might have seemed sinister to most people was intriguing to Pasteur. Chicken cholera had killed over one-tenth of the chicken population in France. The diseased chicken's head had given Pasteur a new challenge: he needed to find and identify the microbes that were causing chicken cholera and use them to find a cure.

BELOW: *An elderly Pasteur leans heavily against his laboratory workbench as he inspects numerous chicken cholera cultures.*

The accident that paid off

Pasteur found that food smeared with cholera microbes from the diseased head and eaten by live chickens killed them. In turn, he found that droppings from infected chickens also spread the disease. Then, an accident brought brilliant results. A culture of cholera microbes was left by accident for a few days. Rather than throw it away, Pasteur decided to inject it into a hen. The next day, to everyone's surprise, the hen was mildly ill, but it was still alive and strutting about its cage. Pasteur then injected more chickens with the days-old culture and was delighted to find that they all lived. The old culture of germs must be weaker than a fresh one. Pasteur's final step was to inject the same chickens with a

WHAT ARE VACCINES?

Pasteur's chicken cholera immunization was revolutionary because it showed that an injection of a weaker strain of the same disease could build up an immunity to the disease. It strengthened a person's or animal's defences against future invasions of the same germ, even if it was a stronger dose. Pasteur had succeeded in turning microbes against themselves. He had to experiment with many different cultures of chicken cholera before he could produce the best vaccine, one that would be weak enough not to kill the chicken, but strong enough to build up the body's immunity to the germs. He found that the longer he left a culture, the weaker it would become. Today, vaccines are produced in controlled laboratory environments, where each culture is carefully prepared in the correct conditions.

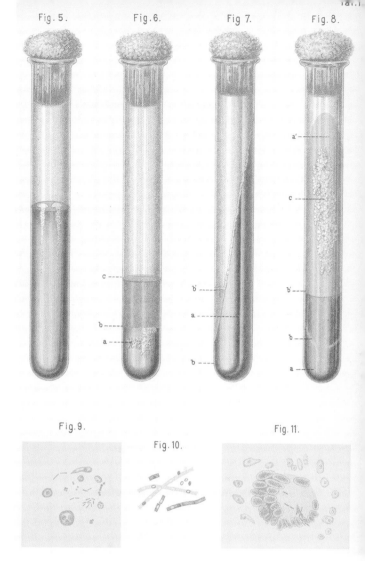

ABOVE: *This drawing, made in 1889, shows test tubes containing the cultures of different human diseases, including pneumonia and tuberculosis. In figures 9 and 11 you can see the microbes viewed under a slide. Pasteur grew cultures of the chicken cholera microbes in the same way.*

fresh culture of the cholera germs – a dose that would usually kill them outright. The chickens all lived. Later, chickens who had not received the old culture were injected with the fatal dose and died – this was proof that the cure worked.

This was a massive breakthrough. Pasteur had struck upon a vaccine for chicken cholera by using a weaker culture of the same disease. Perhaps the same methods could be used to fight other diseases in animals, and possibly even humans.

IN THEIR OWN WORDS

'In the field of experimentation, chance favours the prepared mind.'

PASTEUR, TALKING ABOUT DISCOVERIES
HAPPENING ALMOST BY ACCIDENT.

UNDERSTANDING ANTHRAX

In 1876, a Prussian doctor called Robert Koch identified the germ that caused anthrax, a frightening disease that kills mostly animals, but can kill people. The germ, which was called Bacillus anthracis, is highly contagious and death is swift, sometimes taking just a few hours. The blood of infected animals is clotted and black. In the nineteenth century in France alone, anthrax had wiped out thousands of sheep and cattle. Koch had located the killer microbes in the blood of sick animals. He had also found the microbes in spores.

By 1879, Pasteur had immersed himself in research into the anthrax germ, which was very puzzling. Samples of blood taken from dead animals revealed no deadly microbes, while blood samples from sick animals were teeming with them. For this reason, people doubted that Koch had found the right germ. The other big question was why some animals died, while others escaped anthrax's deathly clutches.

BELOW: *Dr Robert Koch (1843–1910), the Prussian doctor who located the anthrax germ. In 1905, Koch won the Nobel Prize for Medicine for his work on another deadly disease, tuberculosis.*

ANTHRAX BACTERIA

While Pasteur puzzled over the absence of anthrax microbes in the dead bodies of its victims, he found another kind of microbe in its place. The bacteria, which Pasteur named Septic vibrio, lurks in the intestines of all living animals. It is a harmless bacteria which decays the body after death. When something dies, Septic vibrio enters the bloodstream and begins the rotting process. This bacteria behaves quite differently to the anthrax bacteria because it doesn't need oxygen to survive, whereas the anthrax bacteria does. Since there is no oxygen in a dead body, the anthrax bacteria leaves the body as anthrax spores once its victim dies, but Septic vibrio thrives. By finding a reason for the anthrax germ to leave the dead body, Pasteur proved once and for all that it was the anthrax bacteria that killed the animals.

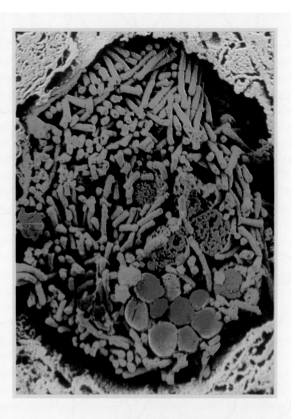

ABOVE: *A cluster of anthrax bacteria in a lung, viewed under a microscope and magnified 810 times.*

The cunning germ

It would take Pasteur the best part of four years to understand anthrax and to prove that Koch had been correct. Painstaking research in the laboratory and out in the field would reveal just how cunning this germ was. Pasteur proved that the germ was transmitted through food and that it was only threatening if an animal had cuts and grazes. The final step was understanding why fields seemed to be infected with anthrax. Pasteur found that diseased animals infected the very ground they were buried in. This was because anthrax spores on the dead bodies were eventually brought back to the surface of the soil by earthworms. In turn, the bacteria would enter the food chain of the cattle, and the cycle was complete.

ABOVE: *A rare photograph of Pasteur in his laboratory at the Ecole Normale in about 1880, when he was fifty-eight, surrounded by flasks, cultures and caged animals used in his experiments.*

LOOKING FOR A CURE

Pasteur now began to look for a cure for anthrax. It wasn't an easy task, but he did have a clue: animals that had eaten infected food and survived seemed to develop a tolerance to anthrax, so he knew that the principle behind his chicken cholera vaccine might work again. However, with chicken cholera, Pasteur had stumbled upon a way of making the bacteria weak enough to work as a vaccine. Anthrax was different. Its bacteria remained strong and aggressive no matter what he did. After months of late nights, the bacteria finally bent to his will. By creating cultures at 42 °C, the bacteria seemed to lose its strength. After successfully testing the vaccine on sheep, Pasteur was ready to tell the world.

In February 1881, he announced to the French Academy of Science that he'd made a vaccine for anthrax. As usual there was doubt, since some people still didn't believe in Pasteur's germ theory of disease. And, as usual, Pasteur wanted to prove to the sceptics that they were wrong.

'…from a purely scientific point of view, the discovery of the vaccine of anthrax constitutes a marked step in advance of that of Jenner's vaccine, since the latter has never been experimentally obtained.'

LOUIS PASTEUR TO THE FRENCH ACADEMY OF SCIENCE, ON 13 JUNE 1881.

ABOVE: *This drawing shows Pasteur performing his anthrax vaccination experiment on sheep at Pouilly-le-Fort on 5 May 1881. 'The twenty-five unvaccinated sheep will all perish. The twenty-five vaccinated sheep will survive,' he promised.*

BELOW: *Pasteur, aged sixty-two, with his wife Marie in 1884.*

The ultimate test

On 5 May 1881, at Pouilly-le-Fort, 40 kilometres from Paris, a massive crowd gathered. Pasteur had set up an experiment involving fifty sheep and ten cows. Half of the animals were vaccinated. It was twelve days before Pasteur injected the animals with another, stronger vaccine. Pasteur then waited until 31 May to administer a large needleful of the deadly anthrax germs to all of the animals. The following hours crawled by. If just one of the vaccinated animals died, Pasteur's reputation would be ruined. The crowds in Pouilly-le-Fort grew bigger. By 1 June the news was not good: one of the sheep had a fever. But by the morning of 2 June, Pasteur could wipe the sweat from his brow. All of his vaccinated animals were alive and well, while those not given the vaccination were dying or already dead. The news spread quickly. Farmers throughout the world wanted Pasteur's miracle cure.

IN THEIR OWN WORDS

'Weary, traversed with deep furrows... the broad forehead wrinkled, seamed with the scars of genius, the mouth slightly drawn by paralysis, but full of kindness, all the more expressive of pity for the suffering of others, as it appears lined by personal sorrow... this is Pasteur as he appeared to me: a conqueror, who will someday become a legend, whose glory is as incalculable as the good he has accomplished.'

PERCY FRANKLAND, WRITING ABOUT HIS FRIEND PASTEUR IN HIS FINAL YEARS.

RABIES — THE FINAL BREAKTHROUGH

Pasteur's final great breakthrough came with his rabies vaccine. In 1885, when Joseph Meister was whisked into his laboratory (see pages 4–5), Pasteur had already been working on a cure for rabies for five years. Rabies was a terrifying disease, which caused an inflammation of the brain, madness, and often a long and dreadful death. Pasteur eventually found the rabies microbes in the nervous system of victims. He finally produced a vaccine using the infected spinal cords of rabbits.

When Joseph Meister arrived, on 6 July 1885, Pasteur wasn't ready to use the vaccine. But the gamble paid off and Joseph survived his awful ordeal. Joseph eventually became a gatekeeper at the Pasteur Institute in Paris, where he worked until his death in old age. He was always grateful to the heroic Monsieur Pasteur, the scientist who had saved his life. Pasteur meanwhile had become world famous. Of all his work, his rabies vaccine brought him the most respect and recognition as a great scientist.

LEFT: *News of Pasteur's rabies vaccine spread quickly around the world. He is seated here with a group of English children who had been bitten by dogs and were sent to him to be given his rabies vaccine. Similar parties of children came to him from all over Europe, including a party of nineteen Russian children who had been bitten by a rabid wolf. Sixteen survived.*

ABOVE: *Pasteur leans against a pillar in one of the spacious and lofty laboratories in the Pasteur Institute, in 1890.*

In the wave of enthusiasm for his rabies vaccine, Pasteur was granted a new laboratory. It was a great honour. The Pasteur Institute, which opened in 1888, would become a base for research into, and cure of, microbial diseases – diseases caused by germs. Despite another more serious stroke in 1887, inner strength and determination saw Pasteur carry on his life's work at the Pasteur Institute until nearly the end of his life. In 1891, he was delighted to hear of the first foreign Pasteur Institute, which was founded in the city of Saigon (now called Hô Chi Minh City), in Vietnam.

In 1894, Pasteur was still working, this time on a diphtheria vaccine. But the years of overwork were finally catching up on the determined old man. In 1895 he was forced to retire and, for the first time in his life, he enjoyed a home life where he could dote on his family, especially his grandchildren. On September 1895, at the age of seventy-two, Pasteur died quietly at home surrounded by his family. After a hero's funeral at Nôtre Dame Cathedral in Paris, he was buried in the chapel at the Pasteur Institute.

RIGHT: *A portrait of Pasteur painted in 1886, with one of his grandchildren. Children were very important to Pasteur as he grew old. In 1887, he said, 'Our only consolation, as we feel our own strength failing us, is to feel that we may help those who come after us…'*

The Legacy of Louis Pasteur

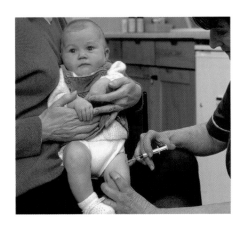

ABOVE: *Vaccines now provide children with protection against dangerous childhood diseases such as diphtheria, whooping cough and rubella.*

LOUIS PASTEUR'S PIONEERING research into germs and the development of vaccines gave future scientists the knowledge and conviction to discover cures for all kinds of diseases. The diphtheria vaccine he started to work on was later developed by his colleague, Dr Roux. Other scientists went on to discover vaccines for hundreds of diseases, including cholera, malaria, tetanus, measles, mumps, flu, hepatitis B, tuberculosis and polio.

Pasteur is also remembered for his sheer determination, showmanship and the willingness to prove his theories outside the laboratory. He managed to capture the imagination of ordinary people and has inspired generations of scientists to prove their theories using experiments.

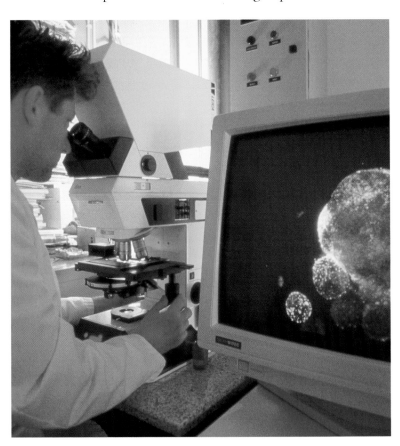

RIGHT: *Scientists use specialized microscopes to view deadly viruses. This researcher is using a microscope to look at human cells carrying the HIV virus, which still has no known cure.*

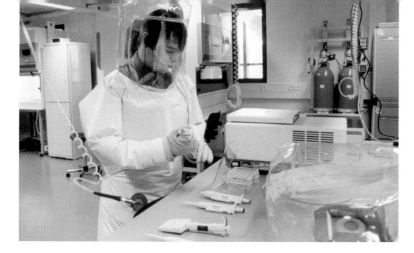

LEFT: *Laboratories have changed a great deal since Pasteur's time. Here, a technician wears special protective clothing as he studies dangerous bacteria and viruses.*

Despite his hero status, there are also critics of Pasteur's work. Some people suggest that he put too much emphasis on the germ theory of disease rather than other causes, such as keeping fit and eating a balanced diet. However, Pasteur also recognized that healthy bodies and a clean environment were equally important in fighting disease and towards the end of his life he said, 'the microbe is nothing, the terrain is everything.' Other people feel he risked too much and criticize his use of human guinea pigs for the rabies vaccine. But in 1915, ten years after Pasteur's death, it was shown that in the case of 6,000 people bitten by rabid dogs, only 0.6 per cent of those inoculated had died, while 16 per cent of those who had not received the vaccine died.

Whatever people think about Pasteur, there is now an international network of Pasteur Institutes which continues to research and develop new vaccines. And there are many challenges to be met. Super bugs and viruses such as AIDS, BSE (Mad Cow Disease) and Ebola have no known cures. Thousands of anonymous scientists are bent over microscopes 100 times more powerful than those used by Pasteur. But they all have the same quest: they hope their discoveries will help to end human suffering.

IN THEIR OWN WORDS

'Young men, have confidence in those powerful and safe methods, of which we do not yet know all the secrets; And, whatever your career may be... do not let yourselves be discouraged by the sadness of certain hours which pass our nations. Live in the serene peace of laboratories and libraries. Say to yourselves first, "What have I done for my instruction?" and, as you gradually advance, "What have I done for my country?" until the time comes when you may have the immense happiness of thinking that you have contributed in some way to the progress and the good of humanity.'

PASTEUR, ADDRESSING STUDENTS AT THE SORBONNE, ON HIS SEVENTIETH BIRTHDAY, 1892.

Timeline

1796

British physician Edward Jenner administers the first vaccination, which is against smallpox.

1822

27 DECEMBER: Louis Pasteur is born in Dôle, France.

1843

Pasteur enters the Ecole Normale Supérieure in fourth place.

1845–48

Famine in Ireland caused when the potato crops failed.

1848

Pasteur discovers that the structures of two forms of crystals are mirror images of each other.

1849

Pasteur becomes Professor of Chemistry at the University of Strasbourg
29 MAY: Pasteur marries Marie Laurent.

1850

The Pasteurs' first daughter Jeanne is born.

1851

The Pasteurs' first son Jean-Baptiste is born.

1853

The Pasteurs' second daughter Cécile is born. Pasteur is awarded the Cross of the Legion of Honour.

1854

Pasteur becomes Professor of Chemistry and Dean of the School of Sciences at Lille. Florence Nightingale, the British nurse, travels to the Crimea (now part of the Ukraine) and cleans up military hospitals on the battlefields of the Crimean War. Her example helps to change attitudes towards patient care.

1856

Pasteur starts to investigate fermentation.

1857

Pasteur becomes Administrator and Director of Scientific Studies at the Ecole Normale in Paris.

1858

The Pasteurs' third daughter Marie-Louise is born.

1859

Pasteur starts his famous work on 'spontaneous generation'. His eldest daughter Jeanne dies from typhoid fever at the age of nine. Charles Darwin's *The Origin of Species* is published.

1862

Pasteur is elected to the French Academy of Sciences.

1863

The last Pasteur child Camille is born.

1864

APRIL: Pasteur presents his germ theory at the Sorbonne in Paris.
SUMMER: He studies fermentation in wine and discovers the process later called pasteurization.

1865

JUNE: Pasteur starts to investigate silkworm diseases. His father suddenly dies.
SEPTEMBER: Pasteur's daughter Camille dies, aged two.
OCTOBER: There is a cholera outbreak in France. Over 200 people a day die in Paris. Pasteur tries to discover the cause but fails.
Sir Joseph Lister (1827–1912) introduces antiseptics after realizing that the formation of pus is due to germs.

1866

MAY: Cécile Pasteur dies from typhoid fever, aged twelve.

1867

Pasteur is appointed Professor of Chemistry at the Sorbonne.

1868

Pasteur finds a way to stop the silkworm diseases.
19 OCTOBER: Pasteur has his first stroke at the age of forty-five.

1870

Pasteur publishes *Studies on the Diseases of Silkworms*.

1870–71

Franco-Prussian War.

1871

Pasteur starts studying beer fermentation.

1873

Pasteur is elected to the Academy of Medicine.

1876

Pasteur publishes his *Studies on Beer*.

1877

Pasteur starts to investigate anthrax.

1878

Pasteur investigates gangrene, septicemia and childbirth fever.

1879

Pasteur discovers how to immunize against disease using weakened bacteria.
His daughter Marie-Louise marries. His son Jean-Baptiste also marries.

1880

Pasteur discovers streptococcus. Starts work on rabies.
Pasteur's first grandchild, Camille Vallery-Radot, is born.

1881

Pasteur discovers an anthrax vaccine. He demonstrates it at Pouilly-le-Fort, outside Paris.

1882

Robert Koch discovers the germ that causes tuberculosis.

1885

Pasteur tries the rabies vaccine on Joseph Meister.

1886

1 MARCH: Pasteur tells the Academy of Sciences that out of 350 people he has treated with his rabies vaccine, only one has died of rabies. Plans are made to build the Pasteur Institute for the treatment of rabies and the study of the transmission of disease.
Pasteur's grandson, Louis Pasteur Vallery-Radot, is born.

1887

Pasteur has his second stroke.

1888

14 NOVEMBER: The Pasteur Institute in Paris is officially opened, with Pasteur as the Director.

1892

27 DECEMBER: Pasteur's seventieth birthday is celebrated in a big ceremony at the Sorbonne, to recognize his achievements.

1894

The Pasteur Institute produces a vaccine for diphtheria.

1895

28 SEPTEMBER: Pasteur dies at his home at Villeneuve l'Etang, surrounded by his family, aged seventy-two.
The diphtheria vaccine is in general use.

1896

Charles Laveran (1845–1922), a French physician, discovers the parasite that causes malaria.

1928

Sir Alexander Fleming (1888–1955), the Scottish biologist, discovers penicillin.

1949

A vaccine for polio is discovered.

1963

Measles vaccine is licensed.

Glossary

Airborne
Carried by the air.

Analyse
To study closely how something is made and what it is made from.

Antiseptic
A substance used to fight and kill germs.

Bacteria
Lots of microbes or micro-organisms, some of which can cause disease.

Biological
To do with plant or animal life.

Blight
A disease, usually of plants. Also used to mean 'destroy'.

Chemical
To do with chemistry, usually made in a laboratory.

Chrysalides
The stage in the life cycle of insects between a larva and an adult.

Code of practice
A set of rules about the way of doing things.

Contagious
A disease that is easily spread from one person or animal to another, usually by contact.

Crystalline
Made of crystals.

Culture
A cultivation of bacteria in a laboratory.

Epidemic
When a disease is caught by many people.

Immunity
When a person or animal is not made ill by germs.

Inflammation
A medical condition where a part of the body becomes swollen, red and hot.

Inoculation
To inject a human or animal with a dose of a disease-causing microbe in order for that person to develop an immunity to that disease.

Manifestation
A change in appearance which is obvious.

Microbe
A germ, or micro-organism, which is too small to be seen by the human eye.

Nervous system
The network of cells within a body which transmit feelings and reactions to the brain.

Paralysis
Loss of movement in the body.

Polarized
The restriction of a passage of light waves to one direction.

Principle
A true fact that is a foundation for other truths.

Sanitation
Maintaining cleanliness and improving conditions to prevent the spread of disease.

Sceptical
To question things, even if they are widely believed.

Spores
Single cells which are capable of developing into a new plant or animal.

Sterilize
To clean something, usually by heat, so it is free of germs.

Tanner
A person who makes animal skins into leather.

Ventilation
To allow air to pass easily through a room or space.

Workaholic
Somebody who is addicted to work.

Zoologist
An expert in the science of animals.

Further Information

BOOKS FOR YOUNGER READERS

Groundbreakers: Louis Pasteur
by Anne Fullick (Heinemann, 2001)

The Cholera Detective
by Dr John Snow (Hodder, 2001)

Livewire Real Lives: Louis Pasteur
(Hodder and Stoughton Educational, 2000)

The Smallpox Slayer
by Alan Brown (Hodder, 2001)

Super Scientists: The Silkworm Mystery
by Pat Thomson (Hodder Wayland, 1998)

BOOKS FOR OLDER READERS

Germ Theory and Its Applications to Medicine
by Louis Pasteur (Prometheus Books, 1996)

An Illustrated History of Medicine
by Jennifer Cochrane (Tiger, 1996)

The Life of Pasteur
by Réne Vallery-Radot
(Constable, 1906, frequently reprinted)

Louis Pasteur: Hunting Killer Germs
by E.A.M Jakob (McGraw Hill, 2000)

The Private Science of Louis Pasteur
by Gerald L. Geison
(Princeton University Press, 1995)

WEBSITES

Nobel e-Museum
www.nobel.se/medicine/articles/jacob
Interesting article about Pasteur and his Institute.

The Woodrow Wilson National Fellowship Foundation
www.woodrow.org/teachers/chemistry/ institutes/1992/Pasteur.html
Fascinating site containing quotes from Pasteur and a timeline of his life.

Hyperlab: France Researchers' Website
http://ambafrance-ca.org/ HYPERLAB/PEOPLE/_pasteur.html
An authoritative site containing a detailed biography of Louis Pasteur.

Famous French Scientists
http://ambafrance- ca.org/HYPERLAB/PEOPLE/_index.html
Information about the life and works of famous French scientists, including Pasteur, Curie and Descartes.

National Inventors Hall of Fame
www.invent.org
Information about Pasteur and other scientists and inventors.

Bright Sparcs Exhibitions: Pasteur in Australia
www.asap.unimelb.edu.au/bsparcs/exhib/ pasteur/pasteur.htm
Information about the work of Pasteur and his Institute in Australia in the late 1800s.

Index

Numbers in **bold** are pages where there is a photograph or an illustration.